Avocado Cookbook

By Brad Hoskinson

Copyright 2025 By Brad Hoskinson. All rights reserved.

No part of this book may be reproduced in any form or by any electronic or mechanical means, including information storage and retrieval systems, without written permission from the author, except for the use of brief quotations in a book review.

Table of Contents

Classic Avocado Toast 7
Avocado and Egg Breakfast Bowl 8
Avocado Omelet 9
Avocado and Bacon Breakfast Wrap 10
Scrambled Eggs with Avocado 11
Avocado Smoothie Bowl 12
Avocado and Spinach Frittata 13
Avocado Pancakes 14
Avocado Chia Pudding 15
Avocado and Banana Smoothie 16
Avocado Caesar Salad 17
Mexican Avocado Corn Salad 18
Avocado and Quinoa Power Bowl 19
Avocado Caprese Salad 20
Avocado and Kale Salad 21
Avocado and Chickpea Salad 22
Avocado Poke Bowl 23
Grilled Avocado and Shrimp Salad 24
Avocado and Black Bean Salad 25
Greek Avocado Salad 26
Classic Guacamole 27
Spicy Mango Guacamole 28
Avocado Hummus 29
Avocado and Yogurt Dip 30
Creamy Avocado Salsa Verde 31
Avocado and Roasted Garlic Dip 32
Avocado and Cilantro Lime Dressing 33

Avocado and White Bean Dip	34
Avocado and Sun-Dried Tomato Spread	35
Avocado and Pesto Spread	36
Turkey and Avocado Sandwich	37
Avocado BLT Sandwich	38
Avocado and Grilled Chicken Wrap	39
Avocado and Smoked Salmon Bagel	40
Avocado and Tuna Salad Sandwich	41
Grilled Cheese with Avocado	42
Caprese Avocado Sandwich	43
Vegan Avocado and Hummus Wrap	44
Roast Beef and Avocado Panini	45
Cucumber and Avocado Tea Sandwich	46
Avocado Shrimp Tacos	47
Grilled Chicken and Avocado Burrito	48
Vegan Avocado Black Bean Tacos	49
Avocado and Fish Tacos	50
Avocado and Beef Quesadilla	51
Spicy Avocado Breakfast Burrito	52
Chipotle Avocado Steak Tacos	53
Creamy Avocado Enchiladas	54
Avocado and Roasted Veggie Tacos	55
Pulled Pork and Avocado Burrito	56
Avocado Pesto Pasta	57
Avocado and Garlic Spaghetti	58
Avocado Alfredo Pasta	59
Avocado and Shrimp Pasta	60
Vegan Creamy Avocado Zoodles	61

Avocado Mac and Cheese 62

Avocado and Lemon Pasta 63

Avocado and Mushroom Carbonara 64

Cold Avocado Soba Noodles 65

Avocado Thai Peanut Noodles 66

Chilled Avocado Cucumber Soup 67

Creamy Avocado and Spinach Soup 68

Spicy Avocado and Corn Soup 69

Avocado and Coconut Milk Soup 70

Mexican Avocado Tortilla Soup 71

Avocado and Black Bean Chili 72

Avocado and Tomato Gazpacho 74

Avocado Miso Soup 75

Avocado and Roasted Pepper Soup 76

Avocado and Chicken Soup 77

Grilled Avocado with Lime and Salt 78

Baked Avocado with Egg 79

Avocado-Stuffed Chicken Breast 80

Roasted Avocado and Sweet Potato 81

Grilled Avocado and Cheese Skewers 82

BBQ Avocado and Corn 83

Avocado-Stuffed Mushrooms 84

Avocado and Halloumi Skewers 85

Baked Avocado Parmesan Fries 86

Grilled Avocado with Honey Glaze 87

Avocado Banana Smoothie 88

Avocado and Chocolate Milkshake 89

Avocado Matcha Latte 90

Avocado and Coconut Smoothie 91
Avocado and Pineapple Juice 92
Iced Avocado Coffee 93
Avocado and Almond Butter Smoothie 94
Avocado and Strawberry Lassi 95
Green Detox Avocado Smoothie 96
Avocado and Chia Milkshake 97
Avocado Chocolate Mousse 98
Avocado and Coconut Ice Cream 99
Avocado Brownies 100
Avocado Cheesecake 101
Avocado and Lime Popsicles 102
Avocado and Banana Muffins 103
Avocado Pancakes with Maple Syrup 104
Avocado and Mango Sorbet 105
Avocado Matcha Cake 106
Avocado and Honey Pudding 107

Classic Avocado Toast

A simple yet delicious breakfast option, Classic Avocado Toast is creamy, flavorful, and packed with healthy fats. Perfect for a quick, nutritious start to your day!

Prep Time: 10 minutes

Ingredients:

- 1 ripe avocado
- 2 slices whole-grain bread
- 1/2 tsp lemon juice
- Salt and pepper to taste
- 1/2 tsp red pepper flakes (optional)
- 1 tbsp olive oil (optional)

Method:

1. Toast the bread slices until golden brown.
2. Cut the avocado in half, remove the pit, and scoop the flesh into a bowl.
3. Mash the avocado with a fork, mixing in lemon juice, salt, and pepper.
4. Spread the mashed avocado evenly onto the toasted bread.
5. Drizzle with olive oil and sprinkle with red pepper flakes if desired.
6. Serve immediately and enjoy!

Avocado and Egg Breakfast Bowl

A hearty and nutritious breakfast bowl featuring creamy avocado, protein-rich eggs, and fresh vegetables for a balanced start to your morning.

Prep Time: 15 minutes

Ingredients:

- ✓ 1 ripe avocado, sliced
- ✓ 2 eggs, cooked to preference (boiled, scrambled, or fried)
- ✓ 1/2 cup cherry tomatoes, halved
- ✓ 1/4 cup red onion, diced
- ✓ 1/2 cup baby spinach
- ✓ 1/2 tsp lemon juice
- ✓ Salt and pepper to taste
- ✓ 1 tbsp olive oil

Method:

1. Arrange baby spinach in a bowl as the base.
2. Slice the avocado and place it in the bowl.
3. Add the cooked eggs, cherry tomatoes, and red onion.
4. Drizzle with olive oil and lemon juice.
5. Season with salt and pepper.
6. Serve immediately and enjoy!

Avocado Omelet

A creamy and nutritious avocado omelet packed with protein, healthy fats, and fresh herbs for a wholesome breakfast.

Prep Time: 15 minutes

Ingredients:

- 2 eggs
- 1/2 ripe avocado, sliced
- 1 tbsp milk (optional)
- 1 tbsp butter or olive oil
- 1/4 cup shredded cheese (cheddar or feta)
- 1 tbsp chopped fresh herbs (parsley or chives)
- Salt and pepper to taste

Method:

1. In a bowl, whisk eggs with milk, salt, and pepper.
2. Heat butter or oil in a skillet over medium heat.
3. Pour in the eggs and let them cook undisturbed until the edges begin to set.
4. Add sliced avocado and cheese to one side of the omelet.
5. Fold the omelet in half and cook for another minute until the cheese melts.
6. Sprinkle with fresh herbs and serve hot.

Avocado and Bacon Breakfast Wrap

A delicious and satisfying wrap filled with creamy avocado, crispy bacon, and scrambled eggs, perfect for breakfast on the go.

Prep Time: 15 minutes

Ingredients:

- 1 large tortilla
- 2 eggs, scrambled
- 2 slices bacon, cooked until crispy
- 1/2 ripe avocado, mashed
- 1/4 cup shredded cheese
- 1 tbsp sour cream (optional)
- Salt and pepper to taste

Method:

1. Warm the tortilla in a dry skillet for 30 seconds.
2. Spread the mashed avocado on the tortilla.
3. Add scrambled eggs, crispy bacon, and shredded cheese.
4. Season with salt and pepper.
5. Roll the tortilla into a wrap and serve warm.

Scrambled Eggs with Avocado

A variation of scrambled eggs, incorporating fresh avocado for a nutritious breakfast option. This delightful dish provides the creamy richness of avocado mixed with the soft texture of scrambled eggs, creating a perfect balance of flavors and nutrients. It's an excellent way to start your day with a healthy and delicious meal that is quick and easy to prepare. Ideal for those who seek both taste and nutrition in their morning routine.

Prep Time: 10 minutes

Ingredients:

- ✓ 2 eggs
- ✓ 1/2 ripe avocado, diced
- ✓ 1 tbsp butter
- ✓ Salt and pepper to taste
- ✓ 1 tbsp fresh herbs (optional)

Method:

1. Whisk the eggs with a pinch of salt and pepper.
2. Heat butter in a pan over medium heat.
3. Pour in the eggs and stir gently until they begin to set.
4. Add the diced avocado and fold into the eggs.
5. Remove from heat and serve immediately, garnished with fresh herbs.

Avocado Smoothie Bowl

A creamy and refreshing smoothie bowl packed with avocado, fruits, and healthy toppings for an energizing breakfast.

Prep Time: 10 minutes

Ingredients:

- ✓ 1/2 ripe avocado
- ✓ 1 frozen banana
- ✓ 1/2 cup Greek yogurt
- ✓ 1/2 cup milk or almond milk
- ✓ 1 tbsp honey or maple syrup
- ✓ Toppings: granola, berries, chia seeds

Method:

1. Blend avocado, banana, yogurt, milk, and honey until smooth.
2. Pour into a bowl and top with granola, berries, and chia seeds.
3. Serve immediately and enjoy!

Avocado and Spinach Frittata

A delicious and nutritious baked frittata with creamy avocado, fresh spinach, and cheese for a satisfying breakfast.

Prep Time: 20 minutes

Ingredients:

- ✓ 4 eggs
- ✓ 1/2 ripe avocado, sliced
- ✓ 1 cup fresh spinach
- ✓ 1/4 cup cheese
- ✓ 1 tbsp olive oil
- ✓ Salt and pepper to taste

Method:

1. Preheat oven to 375°F (190°C).
2. In a bowl, whisk eggs with salt and pepper.
3. Heat oil in an oven-safe pan and sauté spinach.
4. Pour eggs over spinach and top with avocado and cheese.
5. Bake for 12-15 minutes until set.
6. Slice and serve warm.

Avocado Pancakes

Fluffy and nutritious pancakes made with creamy avocado for a unique twist on a breakfast classic.

Prep Time: 20 minutes

Ingredients:

- ✓ 1 ripe avocado
- ✓ 1 cup flour
- ✓ 1 egg
- ✓ 1 cup milk
- ✓ 1 tbsp sugar
- ✓ 1 tsp baking powder
- ✓ 1/2 tsp salt
- ✓ 1 tbsp butter

Method:

1. Blend avocado, egg, milk, and sugar until smooth.
2. In a bowl, mix flour, baking powder, and salt.
3. Combine wet and dry ingredients.
4. Cook pancakes in a buttered pan until golden.
5. Serve with syrup or fruit.

Avocado Chia Pudding

A creamy and healthy pudding made with avocado, chia seeds, and milk for a nutritious start to the day.

Prep Time: 5 minutes + overnight chilling

Ingredients:

- ✓ 1/2 ripe avocado
- ✓ 1 cup milk
- ✓ 3 tbsp chia seeds
- ✓ 1 tbsp honey
- ✓ 1/2 tsp vanilla extract

Method:

1. Blend avocado, milk, honey, and vanilla.
2. Stir in chia seeds and refrigerate overnight.
3. Serve chilled with toppings of choice.

Avocado and Banana Smoothie

A creamy and naturally sweet smoothie with avocado and banana, perfect for a refreshing breakfast.

Prep Time: 5 minutes

Ingredients:

- ✓ 1/2 avocado
- ✓ 1 banana
- ✓ 1 cup milk or almond milk
- ✓ 1 tbsp honey
- ✓ 1/2 tsp cinnamon

Method:

1. Blend all ingredients until smooth.
2. Pour into a glass and enjoy!

Avocado Caesar Salad

A creamy twist on the classic Caesar salad, this version incorporates ripe avocados for a rich and smooth texture. The homemade dressing is lighter but still packed with that signature tangy and garlicky flavor.

> Prep Time: 15 minutes

Ingredients:

- ✓ 2 ripe avocados, sliced
- ✓ 1 large romaine lettuce, chopped
- ✓ 1/2 cup grated Parmesan cheese
- ✓ 1 cup croutons
- ✓ 1 grilled chicken breast, sliced (optional)

For the Dressing:

- ✓ 1 ripe avocado
- ✓ 1/4 cup Greek yogurt
- ✓ 2 tbsp lemon juice
- ✓ 1 tbsp olive oil
- ✓ 1 garlic clove, minced
- ✓ 1 tsp Dijon mustard
- ✓ 1/4 tsp salt
- ✓ 1/4 tsp black pepper

Method:

1. Blend all dressing ingredients until smooth.
2. Toss lettuce with dressing until evenly coated.
3. Add avocado slices, Parmesan, and croutons.
4. Top with grilled chicken if using. Serve immediately.

Mexican Avocado Corn Salad

This vibrant and refreshing salad is bursting with sweet corn, creamy avocado, and bold Mexican flavors. Perfect as a side dish or a light meal.

Prep Time: 20 minutes

Ingredients:

- ✓ 2 ripe avocados, diced
- ✓ 2 cups cooked corn (grilled or boiled)
- ✓ 1 cup cherry tomatoes, halved
- ✓ 1/2 red onion, finely chopped
- ✓ 1/4 cup fresh cilantro, chopped
- ✓ 1 jalapeño, diced (optional)
- ✓ 1/4 cup crumbled cotija cheese (or feta)
- ✓ Juice of 1 lime
- ✓ 1 tbsp olive oil
- ✓ 1/2 tsp salt
- ✓ 1/4 tsp black pepper

Method:

1. In a large bowl, combine all ingredients.
2. Gently toss to mix everything without mashing the avocado.
3. Adjust seasoning and serve immediately.

Avocado and Quinoa Power Bowl

Packed with protein and healthy fats, this avocado and quinoa power bowl is a nutritious and delicious meal perfect for lunch or dinner.

Prep Time: 25 minutes

Ingredients:

- 1 cup cooked quinoa
- 1 ripe avocado, sliced
- 1 cup baby spinach
- 1/2 cup cherry tomatoes, halved
- 1/2 cup chickpeas, drained and rinsed
- 1/4 cup feta cheese, crumbled
- 1 tbsp sunflower seeds

For the Dressing:

- 2 tbsp olive oil
- 1 tbsp lemon juice
- 1 tsp honey
- 1/2 tsp Dijon mustard
- Salt and pepper to taste

Method:

1. In a bowl, arrange quinoa, spinach, tomatoes, chickpeas, avocado, and feta.
2. Whisk together dressing ingredients and drizzle over the salad.
3. Sprinkle with sunflower seeds and serve.

Avocado Caprese Salad

A fresh twist on the classic Caprese salad, this version adds avocado for extra creaminess.

Prep Time: 10 minutes

Ingredients:

- ✓ 2 ripe avocados, sliced
- ✓ 2 large tomatoes, sliced
- ✓ 8 oz fresh mozzarella, sliced
- ✓ 1/4 cup fresh basil leaves
- ✓ 2 tbsp balsamic glaze
- ✓ 1 tbsp olive oil
- ✓ Salt and pepper to taste

Method:

1. Layer avocado, tomato, and mozzarella slices alternately.
2. Drizzle with olive oil and balsamic glaze.
3. Sprinkle with salt, pepper, and fresh basil. Serve immediately.

Avocado and Kale Salad

This salad combines kale with avocado for a nutritious dish. The fresh, crunchy kale leaves provide a solid base packed with vitamins and minerals, while the creamy avocado adds healthy fats and a satisfying texture. To enhance the flavors, you can add a splash of lemon juice, a sprinkle of salt, and some black pepper. Additionally, topping the salad with cherry tomatoes, red onion slices, and a handful of nuts or seeds will contribute more nutrients and elevate the overall taste. This vibrant and wholesome salad is perfect as a light meal on its own or as a side dish to complement your favorite main course.

Prep Time: 15 minutes

Ingredients:

- 2 cups kale, chopped
- 1 ripe avocado, diced
- 1/4 cup almonds, chopped
- 1/4 cup Parmesan cheese, grated
- 1 tbsp lemon juice
- 1 tbsp olive oil
- 1/2 tsp salt

Method:

1. Massage kale with lemon juice and olive oil until tender.
2. Add avocado, almonds, and Parmesan.
3. Toss gently and serve.

Avocado and Chickpea Salad

A protein-rich salad with creamy avocado and hearty chickpeas, perfect for a light meal.

Prep Time: 10 minutes

Ingredients:

- ✓ 1 can chickpeas, drained and rinsed
- ✓ 1 ripe avocado, diced
- ✓ 1/2 red onion, finely chopped
- ✓ 1/4 cup fresh parsley, chopped
- ✓ Juice of 1 lemon
- ✓ 1 tbsp olive oil
- ✓ Salt and pepper to taste

Method:

1. In a bowl, mix chickpeas, avocado, red onion, and parsley.
2. Drizzle with lemon juice and olive oil.
3. Season with salt and pepper. Toss and serve.

Avocado Poke Bowl

A Hawaiian-inspired bowl featuring marinated tuna, avocado, and fresh veggies over rice.

Prep Time: 30 minutes

Ingredients:

- 1 cup cooked sushi rice
- 1 ripe avocado, sliced
- 1/2 lb sushi-grade tuna, diced
- 1/4 cup soy sauce
- 1 tsp sesame oil
- 1/2 tsp sriracha
- 1 tsp sesame seeds
- 1/4 cup cucumber, diced
- 1/4 cup edamame
- 1 tbsp green onions, chopped

Method:

1. Marinate tuna in soy sauce, sesame oil, and sriracha for 10 minutes.
2. Arrange rice in bowls, then top with tuna, avocado, cucumber, and edamame.
3. Sprinkle with sesame seeds and green onions. Serve.

Grilled Avocado and Shrimp Salad

A smoky and flavorful salad with grilled avocado and shrimp, perfect for summer.

Prep Time: 20 minutes

Ingredients:

- 1 ripe avocado, halved and grilled
- 8 shrimp, peeled and deveined
- 2 cups mixed greens
- 1/4 cup cherry tomatoes, halved
- 1 tbsp olive oil
- Juice of 1 lime
- Salt and pepper to taste

Method:

1. Grill avocado halves for 2 minutes per side.
2. Grill shrimp until pink and cooked through.
3. Arrange greens, tomatoes, shrimp, and avocado on a plate.
4. Drizzle with olive oil and lime juice. Serve.

Avocado and Black Bean Salad

A fiber-rich salad combining creamy avocado with hearty black beans.

Prep Time: 10 minutes

Ingredients:

- ✓ 1 can black beans, drained and rinsed
- ✓ 1 ripe avocado, diced
- ✓ 1/2 cup cherry tomatoes, halved
- ✓ 1/4 cup red onion, chopped
- ✓ Juice of 1 lime
- ✓ 1 tbsp olive oil
- ✓ Salt and pepper to taste

Method:

1. Combine all ingredients in a bowl.
2. Toss gently and serve.

Greek Avocado Salad

A Mediterranean-inspired salad with fresh ingredients and creamy avocado.

Prep Time: 10 minutes

Ingredients:

- ✓ 2 ripe avocados, diced
- ✓ 1 cup cucumber, chopped
- ✓ 1/2 cup cherry tomatoes, halved
- ✓ 1/4 cup red onion, thinly sliced
- ✓ 1/4 cup Kalamata olives
- ✓ 1/4 cup feta cheese, crumbled
- ✓ 1 tbsp olive oil
- ✓ 1 tbsp red wine vinegar

Method:

1. Combine all ingredients in a bowl.
2. Toss gently and serve.

Classic Guacamole

A staple in Mexican cuisine, classic guacamole is a creamy, flavorful dip made with ripe avocados, fresh lime juice, and simple seasonings. Perfect for chips, tacos, or as a sandwich spread.

Prep Time: 10 minutes

Ingredients:

- 3 ripe avocados
- 1 small red onion, finely diced
- 1 Roma tomato, diced
- 1 jalapeño, minced (optional)
- 2 tbsp fresh cilantro, chopped
- Juice of 1 lime
- 1/2 tsp salt (or to taste)
- 1/4 tsp ground cumin (optional)

Method:

1. Cut the avocados in half, remove the pit, and scoop out the flesh into a mixing bowl.
2. Mash the avocado with a fork until smooth or chunky, depending on preference.
3. Stir in diced onion, tomato, jalapeño, and cilantro.
4. Squeeze in the lime juice, add salt and cumin (if using), and mix well.
5. Serve immediately with tortilla chips or as a topping for tacos.

Spicy Mango Guacamole

This guacamole variation adds a tropical twist with sweet mango and a spicy kick from jalapeños, making it an exciting dip or topping.

Prep Time: 15 minutes

Ingredients:

- ✓ 3 ripe avocados
- ✓ 1 small mango, diced
- ✓ 1/2 red onion, finely chopped
- ✓ 1 small jalapeño, minced
- ✓ 2 tbsp fresh cilantro, chopped
- ✓ Juice of 1 lime
- ✓ 1/2 tsp salt
- ✓ 1/4 tsp chili powder

Method:

1. Mash the avocados in a bowl to your desired consistency.
2. Mix in mango, onion, jalapeño, and cilantro.
3. Add lime juice, salt, and chili powder. Stir well.
4. Serve with chips or as a topping for grilled meats or tacos.

Avocado Hummus

A creamy, nutritious dip combining the flavors of hummus and avocado for a smooth, flavorful spread.

Prep Time: 10 minutes

Ingredients:

- 1 ripe avocado
- 1 can (15 oz) chickpeas, drained and rinsed
- 2 tbsp tahini
- 2 tbsp olive oil
- Juice of 1 lemon
- 1 clove garlic, minced
- 1/2 tsp cumin
- 1/2 tsp salt
- 2 tbsp water (if needed for consistency)

Method:

1. Blend all ingredients in a food processor until smooth.
2. Add water as needed for a creamy consistency.
3. Serve with pita chips or fresh veggies.

Avocado and Yogurt Dip

A tangy and creamy dip with Greek yogurt and avocado, perfect for pairing with veggies or pita.

Prep Time: 5 minutes

Ingredients:

- 1 ripe avocado
- 1/2 cup Greek yogurt
- 1 tbsp lemon juice
- 1 garlic clove, minced
- 1/2 tsp salt
- 1 tbsp fresh dill or parsley, chopped

Method:

1. Mash the avocado and mix with Greek yogurt.
2. Stir in lemon juice, garlic, salt, and herbs.
3. Serve chilled.

Creamy Avocado Salsa Verde

A smooth and tangy salsa made with roasted tomatillos and avocado, great for tacos and nachos.

Prep Time: 10 minutes

Ingredients:

- ✓ 4 tomatillos, husked and rinsed
- ✓ 1 avocado
- ✓ 1 garlic clove
- ✓ 1/2 cup fresh cilantro
- ✓ Juice of 1 lime
- ✓ 1/2 tsp salt

Method:

1. Blend all ingredients in a food processor until smooth.
2. Adjust seasoning and serve immediately.

Avocado and Roasted Garlic Dip

A rich, garlicky dip with a smooth avocado base.

Prep Time: 10 minutes

Ingredients:

- ✓ 1 avocado
- ✓ 1 head of garlic, roasted
- ✓ 2 tbsp olive oil
- ✓ 1/2 tsp salt

Method:

1. Squeeze roasted garlic into a bowl and mash.
2. Add avocado, olive oil, and salt, and blend until smooth.
3. Serve with crackers or bread.

Avocado and Cilantro Lime Dressing

A creamy, zesty dressing ideal for salads and grain bowls.

Prep Time: 5 minutes

Ingredients:

- ✓ 1 avocado
- ✓ 1/2 cup fresh cilantro
- ✓ Juice of 2 limes
- ✓ 1/4 cup olive oil
- ✓ 1 garlic clove
- ✓ 1/4 tsp salt

Method:

1. Blend all ingredients until smooth.
2. Adjust seasoning and drizzle over salads.

Avocado and White Bean Dip

A protein-rich dip with a smooth texture and fresh flavors.

Prep Time: 10 minutes

Ingredients:

- ✓ 1 avocado
- ✓ 1 can (15 oz) white beans, drained and rinsed
- ✓ 2 tbsp lemon juice
- ✓ 1 garlic clove
- ✓ 1/4 cup olive oil
- ✓ 1/2 tsp salt

Method:

1. Blend all ingredients until creamy.
2. Serve with vegetables or crackers.

Avocado and Sun-Dried Tomato Spread

A rich, umami-packed spread for sandwiches and crackers.

Prep Time: 10 minutes

Ingredients:

- ✓ 1 avocado
- ✓ 1/4 cup sun-dried tomatoes, chopped
- ✓ 1 tbsp olive oil
- ✓ 1/2 tsp salt

Method:

1. Mash the avocado and mix with sun-dried tomatoes, olive oil, and salt.
2. Use as a spread or dip.

Avocado and Pesto Spread

A creamy spread combining fresh basil pesto with avocado, perfect for sandwiches and pasta.

Prep Time: 5 minutes

Ingredients:

- ✓ 1 avocado
- ✓ 2 tbsp basil pesto
- ✓ 1 tbsp lemon juice

Method:

1. Mash the avocado and mix with pesto and lemon juice.
2. Spread on toast or mix with pasta.

Turkey and Avocado Sandwich

This turkey and avocado sandwich is a fresh and hearty option, combining tender turkey slices, creamy avocado, and crisp veggies for a satisfying meal.

Prep Time: 10 minutes

Ingredients:

- ✓ 2 slices whole grain bread
- ✓ 4 oz sliced turkey breast
- ✓ 1/2 avocado, mashed
- ✓ 1 slice Swiss or cheddar cheese
- ✓ 2 lettuce leaves
- ✓ 2 slices tomato
- ✓ 1 tbsp mayonnaise or mustard

Method:

1. Spread mashed avocado on one slice of bread and mayonnaise or mustard on the other.
2. Layer turkey, cheese, lettuce, and tomato on top.
3. Close the sandwich, slice in half, and serve.

Avocado BLT Sandwich

A twist on the classic BLT, this sandwich features creamy avocado for extra flavor and texture.

Prep Time: 10 minutes

Ingredients:

- ✓ 2 slices sourdough or whole wheat bread
- ✓ 4 slices crispy bacon
- ✓ 1/2 avocado, sliced
- ✓ 2 slices tomato
- ✓ 2 lettuce leaves
- ✓ 1 tbsp mayonnaise

Method:

1. Toast the bread and spread mayonnaise on one side.
2. Layer bacon, avocado slices, tomato, and lettuce.
3. Close the sandwich, slice, and serve.

Avocado and Grilled Chicken Wrap

This wrap is packed with grilled chicken, avocado, and fresh vegetables, making it a great meal on the go.

Prep Time: 15 minutes

Ingredients:

- ✓ 2 large tortillas
- ✓ 1 grilled chicken breast, sliced
- ✓ 1 avocado, sliced
- ✓ 1/4 cup shredded cheese
- ✓ 1/2 cup mixed greens
- ✓ 2 tbsp ranch dressing

Method:

1. Warm the tortillas slightly for easy folding.
2. Layer chicken, avocado, cheese, and greens in the center.
3. Drizzle with ranch dressing, fold the sides in, and roll tightly.
4. Slice in half and serve.

Avocado and Smoked Salmon Bagel

This elegant and delicious bagel combines creamy avocado with rich smoked salmon for a gourmet breakfast or lunch.

Prep Time: 10 minutes

Ingredients:

- ✓ 1 bagel, halved and toasted
- ✓ 2 oz smoked salmon
- ✓ 1/2 avocado, mashed
- ✓ 1 tbsp cream cheese
- ✓ 1 tbsp red onion, thinly sliced
- ✓ 1 tsp capers
- ✓ 1 tsp fresh dill

Method:

1. Spread cream cheese on one bagel half and mashed avocado on the other.
2. Layer smoked salmon, red onion, and capers.
3. Sprinkle with fresh dill, close the bagel, and serve.

Avocado and Tuna Salad Sandwich

This creamy avocado and tuna salad sandwich is a nutritious and delicious alternative to traditional tuna salad.

Prep Time: 10 minutes

Ingredients:

- ✓ 2 slices whole wheat bread
- ✓ 1 can (5 oz) tuna, drained
- ✓ 1/2 avocado, mashed
- ✓ 1 tbsp Greek yogurt or mayonnaise
- ✓ 1/4 cup diced celery
- ✓ 1 tbsp lemon juice
- ✓ 1/4 tsp salt
- ✓ 1/4 tsp black pepper

Method:

1. In a bowl, mix tuna, avocado, yogurt, celery, lemon juice, salt, and pepper.
2. Spread the mixture onto one slice of bread.
3. Top with another slice, cut in half, and serve.

Grilled Cheese with Avocado

A creamy and cheesy twist on the classic grilled cheese sandwich.

Prep Time: 10 minutes

Ingredients:

- ✓ 2 slices sourdough bread
- ✓ 1/2 avocado, mashed
- ✓ 2 slices cheddar cheese
- ✓ 1 tbsp butter

Method:

1. Spread avocado on one slice of bread and top with cheese.
2. Close the sandwich and butter the outer sides.
3. Grill in a skillet over medium heat until golden brown on both sides.
4. Slice and serve warm.

Caprese Avocado Sandwich

This fresh and flavorful sandwich features avocado, mozzarella, tomatoes, and basil.

Prep Time: 10 minutes

Ingredients:

- 2 slices ciabatta or sourdough bread
- 1/2 avocado, mashed
- 2 slices fresh mozzarella
- 2 slices tomato
- 2 fresh basil leaves
- 1 tsp balsamic glaze

Method:

1. Spread mashed avocado on one slice of bread.
2. Layer mozzarella, tomato, and basil.
3. Drizzle with balsamic glaze, close the sandwich, and serve.

Vegan Avocado and Hummus Wrap

A nutritious and plant-based wrap packed with creamy avocado and hummus.

Prep Time: 10 minutes

Ingredients:

- ✓ 2 large tortillas
- ✓ 1/2 cup hummus
- ✓ 1 avocado, sliced
- ✓ 1/2 cup shredded carrots
- ✓ 1/2 cup baby spinach
- ✓ 1 tbsp lemon juice

Method:

1. Spread hummus on each tortilla.
2. Layer avocado, carrots, and spinach.
3. Drizzle with lemon juice and roll up tightly.
4. Slice in half and serve.

Roast Beef and Avocado Panini

This warm, crispy panini combines juicy roast beef and creamy avocado for a hearty sandwich.

Prep Time: 15 minutes

Ingredients:

- ✓ 2 ciabatta rolls
- ✓ 4 oz roast beef
- ✓ 1/2 avocado, sliced
- ✓ 2 slices provolone cheese
- ✓ 1 tbsp horseradish mayo
- ✓ 1 tbsp butter

Method:

1. Spread horseradish mayo on the bread.
2. Layer roast beef, avocado, and cheese.
3. Close the sandwich and butter the outer sides.
4. Grill in a panini press or skillet until golden and crisp.
5. Serve warm.

Cucumber and Avocado Tea Sandwich

A light and refreshing tea sandwich perfect for afternoon tea or a snack.

Prep Time: 10 minutes

Ingredients:

- ✓ 4 slices white or whole wheat bread
- ✓ 1/2 avocado, mashed
- ✓ 1/4 cup cream cheese
- ✓ 1/2 cucumber, thinly sliced
- ✓ 1 tbsp fresh dill

Method:

1. Mix mashed avocado with cream cheese.
2. Spread on bread slices and layer with cucumber.
3. Sprinkle with fresh dill and close the sandwich.
4. Trim the crusts, cut into small squares or triangles, and serve.

Avocado Shrimp Tacos

These shrimp tacos are fresh, flavorful, and perfectly complemented by creamy avocado. A quick and easy meal for taco lovers!

Prep Time: 20 minutes

Ingredients:

- 1 lb shrimp, peeled and deveined
- 1 tbsp olive oil
- 1 tsp chili powder
- 1/2 tsp garlic powder
- 1/2 tsp cumin
- 1/4 tsp salt
- 8 small corn tortillas
- 1 avocado, diced
- 1/2 cup shredded cabbage
- 1/4 cup chopped cilantro
- 1/4 cup crumbled cotija cheese (optional)
- 1 lime, cut into wedges

Method:

1. Heat olive oil in a skillet over medium heat.
2. Toss shrimp with chili powder, garlic powder, cumin, and salt.
3. Cook shrimp for 2–3 minutes per side until opaque.
4. Warm tortillas and assemble with shrimp, avocado, cabbage, and cilantro.
5. Sprinkle with cotija cheese and serve with lime wedges.

Grilled Chicken and Avocado Burrito

A hearty and delicious burrito filled with juicy grilled chicken, creamy avocado, and fresh toppings.

Prep Time: 25 minutes

Ingredients:

- ✓ 2 large tortillas
- ✓ 1 grilled chicken breast, sliced
- ✓ 1 avocado, sliced
- ✓ 1/2 cup cooked rice
- ✓ 1/4 cup black beans
- ✓ 1/4 cup shredded cheese
- ✓ 2 tbsp salsa
- ✓ 1 tbsp sour cream

Method:

1. Warm tortillas in a dry pan.
2. Layer rice, black beans, chicken, avocado, cheese, and salsa in the center.
3. Fold in the sides and roll up tightly.
4. Grill the burrito in a pan until golden and serve.

Vegan Avocado Black Bean Tacos

A simple and delicious vegan taco filled with black beans, creamy avocado, and fresh veggies.

Prep Time: 15 minutes

Ingredients:

1. 8 small corn tortillas
2. 1 can (15 oz) black beans, drained and rinsed
3. 1 avocado, sliced
4. 1/2 cup shredded lettuce
5. 1/2 cup diced tomatoes
6. 1/4 cup chopped red onion
7. 1/4 cup cilantro
8. 1 tsp lime juice

Method:

1. Warm tortillas in a dry pan.
2. Heat black beans and mash slightly.
3. Assemble tacos with black beans, avocado, lettuce, tomatoes, and onion.
4. Garnish with cilantro and a squeeze of lime.

Avocado and Fish Tacos

These fish tacos are light, flavorful, and enhanced by creamy avocado.

Prep Time: 20 minutes

Ingredients:

- 1 lb white fish (tilapia or cod), cut into strips
- 1 tbsp olive oil
- 1/2 tsp paprika
- 1/2 tsp garlic powder
- 8 small tortillas
- 1 avocado, diced
- 1/2 cup shredded cabbage
- 1/4 cup sour cream
- 1 lime, cut into wedges

Method:

1. Season fish with paprika and garlic powder.
2. Cook in a skillet with olive oil for 3–4 minutes per side.
3. Warm tortillas and assemble with fish, avocado, cabbage, and sour cream.
4. Serve with lime wedges.

Avocado and Beef Quesadilla

A crispy quesadilla filled with seasoned beef, melted cheese, and creamy avocado.

Prep Time: 20 minutes

Ingredients:

- ✓ 2 large flour tortillas
- ✓ 1/2 lb ground beef
- ✓ 1/2 tsp taco seasoning
- ✓ 1 avocado, sliced
- ✓ 1 cup shredded cheese
- ✓ 1 tbsp butter

Method:

1. Cook beef with taco seasoning until browned.
2. Spread beef, cheese, and avocado on one tortilla.
3. Top with another tortilla and cook in a buttered skillet until golden.
4. Slice and serve.

Spicy Avocado Breakfast Burrito

A flavorful breakfast burrito packed with eggs, avocado, and a spicy kick.

Prep Time: 15 minutes

Ingredients:

- ✓ 2 large tortillas
- ✓ 4 eggs, scrambled
- ✓ 1 avocado, sliced
- ✓ 1/4 cup shredded cheese
- ✓ 1/4 cup cooked chorizo or spicy sausage
- ✓ 1 tbsp hot sauce

Method:

1. Warm tortillas and layer scrambled eggs, chorizo, avocado, and cheese.
2. Drizzle with hot sauce, fold, and roll into a burrito.
3. Serve warm.

Chipotle Avocado Steak Tacos

These smoky chipotle steak tacos are bold in flavor and perfectly balanced with creamy avocado.

Prep Time: 30 minutes

Ingredients:

- 1 lb steak (flank or skirt)
- 1 tbsp chipotle seasoning
- 8 small tortillas
- 1 avocado, diced
- 1/4 cup chopped onion
- 1/4 cup chopped cilantro
- 1 lime, cut into wedges

Method:

1. Season steak with chipotle seasoning and grill to desired doneness.
2. Slice thinly and assemble tacos with steak, avocado, onion, and cilantro.
3. Serve with lime wedges.

Creamy Avocado Enchiladas

These enchiladas are rich and creamy, filled with avocado and smothered in a delicious sauce.

Prep Time: 30 minutes

Ingredients:

- 8 small tortillas
- 2 cups cooked shredded chicken
- 1 avocado, mashed
- 1 cup shredded cheese
- 1 cup enchilada sauce
- 1/4 cup sour cream

Method:

1. Mix chicken, mashed avocado, and half the cheese.
2. Fill tortillas, roll, and place in a baking dish.
3. Pour enchilada sauce over the top and sprinkle with remaining cheese.
4. Bake at 375°F (190°C) for 15 minutes and serve with sour cream.

Avocado and Roasted Veggie Tacos

A flavorful vegetarian taco with roasted veggies and creamy avocado.

Prep Time: 30 minutes

Ingredients:

- ✓ 1 zucchini, sliced
- ✓ 1 bell pepper, sliced
- ✓ 1/2 onion, sliced
- ✓ 1 tbsp olive oil
- ✓ 8 small tortillas
- ✓ 1 avocado, sliced
- ✓ 1/4 cup feta cheese (optional)

Method:

1. Roast vegetables at 400°F (200°C) for 20 minutes.
2. Warm tortillas and assemble with roasted veggies and avocado.
3. Top with feta cheese and serve.

Pulled Pork and Avocado Burrito

A hearty burrito filled with tender pulled pork and creamy avocado.

Prep Time: 10 minutes (plus slow cooking time for pork)

Ingredients:

- ✓ 2 large tortillas
- ✓ 1 cup pulled pork
- ✓ 1 avocado, sliced
- ✓ 1/2 cup cooked rice
- ✓ 1/4 cup black beans
- ✓ 1/4 cup shredded cheese

Method:

1. Warm tortillas and layer rice, beans, pulled pork, avocado, and cheese.
2. Fold and roll into a burrito.
3. Grill in a pan for extra crispiness.

Avocado Pesto Pasta

This creamy, flavorful avocado pesto pasta is a fresh twist on the classic pesto dish. The avocado replaces traditional cream to create a rich, smooth sauce that coats every strand of pasta, with the freshness of basil and the zing of garlic. It's the perfect combination of healthy fats and Italian flavor!

Prep Time: 15 minutes

Ingredients:

- ✓ 1 ripe avocado
- ✓ 2 cups fresh basil leaves
- ✓ 1/4 cup pine nuts (or walnuts)
- ✓ 2 cloves garlic
- ✓ 1/2 cup grated Parmesan cheese
- ✓ 2 tbsp olive oil
- ✓ 1 tbsp lemon juice
- ✓ Salt and pepper to taste
- ✓ 400g pasta of choice

Method:

1. Cook the pasta according to the package instructions. Drain and set aside.
2. In a food processor, combine the avocado, basil, pine nuts, garlic, Parmesan, olive oil, lemon juice, salt, and pepper. Process until smooth.
3. Toss the cooked pasta with the avocado pesto until well coated.
4. Serve with extra Parmesan and a drizzle of olive oil, if desired.

Avocado and Garlic Spaghetti

This avocado and garlic spaghetti is a creamy, garlic-infused pasta dish that's light yet flavorful. The combination of ripe avocado and garlic creates a delightful sauce that's both rich and savory, perfect for a quick and satisfying meal.

Prep Time: 10 minutes

Ingredients:

- ✓ 1 ripe avocado
- ✓ 2 cloves garlic, minced
- ✓ 200g spaghetti
- ✓ 2 tbsp olive oil
- ✓ 1 tbsp lemon juice
- ✓ Salt and pepper to taste
- ✓ Fresh parsley, chopped (optional)

Method:

1. Cook the spaghetti according to the package instructions. Drain and set aside, reserving some pasta water.
2. In a pan, heat the olive oil over medium heat. Add the garlic and sauté for about 1-2 minutes until fragrant.
3. In a blender or food processor, combine the avocado, garlic, lemon juice, salt, and pepper. Blend until smooth.
4. Toss the spaghetti with the avocado sauce, adding reserved pasta water to adjust the consistency.
5. Garnish with chopped parsley before serving.

Avocado Alfredo Pasta

This Avocado Alfredo Pasta combines the richness of traditional Alfredo sauce with the creamy texture of avocado. It's a guilt-free, comforting pasta dish that's perfect for any occasion.

Prep Time: 15 minutes

Ingredients:

- ✓ 1 ripe avocado
- ✓ 1/2 cup unsweetened almond milk or regular milk
- ✓ 1/4 cup grated Parmesan cheese
- ✓ 2 cloves garlic
- ✓ 2 tbsp olive oil
- ✓ 400g pasta of choice
- ✓ Salt and pepper to taste

Method:

1. Cook the pasta according to the package instructions. Drain and set aside.
2. In a food processor, combine the avocado, almond milk, Parmesan, garlic, olive oil, salt, and pepper. Blend until smooth and creamy.
3. Toss the cooked pasta with the avocado Alfredo sauce until well coated.
4. Serve with additional Parmesan and black pepper if desired.

Avocado and Shrimp Pasta

This creamy avocado and shrimp pasta is a perfect combination of flavors. The buttery avocado pairs perfectly with the sweetness of shrimp, creating a luxurious pasta dish that's sure to impress.

Prep Time: 20 minutes

Ingredients:

- ✓ 1 ripe avocado
- ✓ 200g shrimp, peeled and deveined
- ✓ 2 cloves garlic, minced
- ✓ 1 tbsp olive oil
- ✓ 400g pasta of choice
- ✓ 1 tbsp lemon juice
- ✓ Salt and pepper to taste
- ✓ Fresh parsley, chopped (optional)

Method:

1. Cook the pasta according to the package instructions. Drain and set aside.
2. In a pan, heat olive oil over medium heat. Add garlic and shrimp, cooking for 3-4 minutes until the shrimp is pink and cooked through. Remove from heat.
3. In a food processor, combine the avocado, lemon juice, salt, and pepper. Blend until smooth.
4. Toss the cooked pasta with the avocado sauce and shrimp until well combined.
5. Garnish with fresh parsley and serve.

Vegan Creamy Avocado Zoodles

This vegan creamy avocado zoodles recipe is a light and healthy alternative to traditional pasta. The creamy avocado sauce pairs beautifully with zucchini noodles for a fresh, low-carb meal that's full of flavor.

Prep Time: 10 minutes

Ingredients:

- 2 medium zucchinis, spiralized into zoodles
- 1 ripe avocado
- 1 tbsp lemon juice
- 2 tbsp olive oil
- 2 cloves garlic
- Salt and pepper to taste
- Fresh basil, chopped (optional)

Method:

1. Spiralize the zucchinis into zoodles and set aside.
2. In a blender or food processor, combine the avocado, lemon juice, olive oil, garlic, salt, and pepper. Blend until smooth.
3. Toss the zoodles with the creamy avocado sauce until well coated.
4. Garnish with fresh basil and serve.

Avocado Mac and Cheese

This creamy avocado mac and cheese is a healthier take on the classic comfort food. The creamy avocado replaces the heavy cream, giving the dish a rich texture with a subtle avocado flavor.

Prep Time: 20 minutes

Ingredients:

- ✓ 1 ripe avocado
- ✓ 1 cup shredded cheddar cheese
- ✓ 1/2 cup milk
- ✓ 1 tbsp butter
- ✓ 1/2 tsp garlic powder
- ✓ 200g elbow macaroni
- ✓ Salt and pepper to taste

Method:

1. Cook the macaroni according to the package instructions. Drain and set aside.
2. In a pan, melt the butter over medium heat. Add the garlic powder and milk, stirring until combined.
3. In a food processor, blend the avocado until smooth. Add the avocado to the milk mixture and stir until well combined.
4. Add the shredded cheddar cheese to the pan and cook until melted.
5. Toss the cooked macaroni with the avocado cheese sauce until well coated.
6. Serve immediately.

Avocado and Lemon Pasta

This avocado and lemon pasta is a light, fresh, and creamy dish that's perfect for any season. The avocado creates a smooth and velvety sauce, while the lemon adds a zesty twist.

Prep Time: 15 minutes

Ingredients:

- ✓ 1 ripe avocado
- ✓ 1 tbsp lemon juice
- ✓ 2 cloves garlic
- ✓ 400g pasta of choice
- ✓ 2 tbsp olive oil
- ✓ Salt and pepper to taste

Method:

1. Cook the pasta according to the package instructions. Drain and set aside.
2. In a food processor, combine the avocado, lemon juice, garlic, olive oil, salt, and pepper. Blend until smooth.
3. Toss the cooked pasta with the avocado sauce until well coated.
4. Serve with a sprinkle of lemon zest for extra flavor.

Avocado and Mushroom Carbonara

This avocado and mushroom carbonara is a rich and creamy twist on the classic carbonara. The avocado gives the sauce a silky smooth texture, while the mushrooms add depth and earthy flavor.

Prep Time: 20 minutes

Ingredients:

- 1 ripe avocado
- 200g mushrooms, sliced
- 2 eggs
- 400g pasta of choice
- 2 cloves garlic, minced
- 1/4 cup Parmesan cheese
- Salt and pepper to taste
- Olive oil for cooking

Method:

1. Cook the pasta according to the package instructions. Drain and set aside.
2. In a pan, heat olive oil over medium heat. Add the mushrooms and garlic, cooking until the mushrooms are tender.
3. In a bowl, whisk together the eggs, Parmesan, salt, and pepper.
4. In a food processor, blend the avocado until smooth.
5. Toss the cooked pasta with the avocado, egg mixture, and mushrooms. The heat from the pasta will cook the eggs, creating a creamy sauce.
6. Serve with extra Parmesan and black pepper.

Cold Avocado Soba Noodles

This cold avocado soba noodles dish is a refreshing and light meal that's perfect for warmer weather. The creamy avocado dressing pairs perfectly with the nutty soba noodles for a flavorful, satisfying dish.

Prep Time: 15 minutes

Ingredients:

- ✓ 200g soba noodles
- ✓ 1 ripe avocado
- ✓ 1 tbsp soy sauce
- ✓ 1 tbsp rice vinegar
- ✓ 1 tsp sesame oil
- ✓ 1 tbsp sesame seeds
- ✓ 2 green onions, chopped

Method:

1. Cook the soba noodles according to the package instructions. Drain and rinse under cold water.
2. In a blender, combine the avocado, soy sauce, rice vinegar, and sesame oil. Blend until smooth.
3. Toss the soba noodles with the avocado dressing.
4. Garnish with sesame seeds and chopped green onions before serving.

Avocado Thai Peanut Noodles

This avocado Thai peanut noodle dish is a creamy and flavorful twist on the traditional Thai peanut noodles. The avocado adds a rich texture to the peanut sauce, making it even more delicious.

Prep Time: 15 minutes

Ingredients:

- 200g rice noodles
- 1 ripe avocado
- 3 tbsp peanut butter
- 1 tbsp soy sauce
- 1 tbsp lime juice
- 1 tbsp honey
- 2 cloves garlic, minced
- 1 tsp ginger, grated
- 1 tbsp sesame oil
- Chopped peanuts for garnish

Method:

1. Cook the rice noodles according to the package instructions. Drain and set aside.
2. In a blender, combine the avocado, peanut butter, soy sauce, lime juice, honey, garlic, ginger, and sesame oil. Blend until smooth.
3. Toss the noodles with the avocado peanut sauce until well coated.
4. Garnish with chopped peanuts and serve.

Chilled Avocado Cucumber Soup

This refreshing and creamy chilled avocado cucumber soup is perfect for warm days. It's light, healthy, and packed with flavors, making it an excellent appetizer or a light meal. The cool, smooth texture combined with a hint of lemon and garlic creates a delicious balance.

Prep Time: 15 minutes

Ingredients:

- 2 ripe avocados, peeled and pitted
- 1 large cucumber, peeled and chopped
- 1/4 cup fresh cilantro
- 1/2 cup plain Greek yogurt
- 1/2 cup vegetable broth or water
- 2 tbsp lime juice
- 1 garlic clove, minced
- 1/2 tsp ground cumin
- Salt and pepper, to taste
- Ice cubes (optional, for extra chill)
- Fresh cilantro or mint leaves for garnish

Method:

1. In a blender, combine the avocados, cucumber, cilantro, Greek yogurt, vegetable broth, lime juice, garlic, cumin, salt, and pepper.
2. Blend until smooth and creamy. If the soup is too thick, add a little more vegetable broth or water to reach your desired consistency.
3. Taste and adjust the seasoning if needed.
4. Chill the soup in the fridge for at least 30 minutes before serving.
5. Serve chilled, garnished with fresh cilantro or mint leaves and ice cubes if desired.

Creamy Avocado and Spinach Soup

This creamy avocado and spinach soup is a delicious blend of nutritious greens and creamy avocado. It's comforting and satisfying while still being light. The fresh spinach adds a lovely color and earthy flavor that complements the smoothness of the avocado.

Prep Time: 10 minutes

Ingredients:

- ✓ 2 ripe avocados, peeled and pitted
- ✓ 2 cups fresh spinach, packed
- ✓ 1/2 cup coconut milk (or any preferred milk)
- ✓ 1/2 cup vegetable broth
- ✓ 1 small onion, chopped
- ✓ 1 garlic clove, minced
- ✓ 1 tbsp olive oil
- ✓ 1 tbsp lemon juice
- ✓ Salt and pepper, to taste

Method:

1. Heat the olive oil in a medium saucepan over medium heat. Add the chopped onion and garlic and sauté for 3-4 minutes until soft and fragrant.
2. Add the spinach to the saucepan and cook until wilted, about 2 minutes.
3. Add the vegetable broth and bring to a simmer. Let it cook for 5 minutes.
4. Remove the saucepan from the heat and let it cool slightly.
5. In a blender, combine the avocado, cooked spinach mixture, coconut milk, lemon juice, salt, and pepper.
6. Blend until smooth and creamy. Adjust seasoning as needed.
7. Serve warm or chilled, depending on your preference.

Spicy Avocado and Corn Soup

A delightful spicy avocado and corn soup that combines creamy avocado with the sweetness of corn and a bit of heat from jalapeños. This soup is perfect for those who love bold flavors with a smooth texture.

> Prep Time: 15 minutes

Ingredients:

- ✓ 2 ripe avocados, peeled and pitted
- ✓ 1 cup corn kernels (fresh, frozen, or canned)
- ✓ 1 small onion, chopped
- ✓ 1 jalapeño pepper, seeds removed and chopped
- ✓ 2 cups vegetable broth
- ✓ 1/2 cup coconut milk
- ✓ 1 tbsp lime juice
- ✓ 1 garlic clove, minced
- ✓ 1/2 tsp cumin
- ✓ Salt and pepper, to taste
- ✓ Fresh cilantro, for garnish

Method:

1. In a medium pot, heat a little olive oil over medium heat. Add the chopped onion and jalapeño, and cook until softened, about 4-5 minutes.
2. Add the garlic and corn to the pot, and cook for an additional 2 minutes.
3. Pour in the vegetable broth and coconut milk. Bring the mixture to a simmer and cook for 5-7 minutes.
4. Remove from heat and let cool slightly.
5. In a blender, combine the avocado, cooked corn mixture, lime juice, cumin, salt, and pepper. Blend until smooth and creamy.
6. Taste and adjust the seasoning if needed.
7. Serve warm or chilled, garnished with fresh cilantro.

Avocado and Coconut Milk Soup

A velvety, tropical soup made with creamy avocado and coconut milk. This soup is rich, satisfying, and perfect for cozy nights or as a light lunch.

Prep Time: 10 minutes

Ingredients:

- ✓ 2 ripe avocados, peeled and pitted
- ✓ 1 cup coconut milk
- ✓ 1 cup vegetable broth
- ✓ 1 small onion, chopped
- ✓ 1 garlic clove, minced
- ✓ 1 tbsp olive oil
- ✓ 1 tbsp lime juice
- ✓ Salt and pepper, to taste
- ✓ Fresh cilantro, for garnish

Method:

1. Heat olive oil in a medium pot over medium heat. Add the chopped onion and garlic, cooking for 3-4 minutes until soft.
2. Add the vegetable broth and coconut milk to the pot. Bring to a simmer and cook for 5 minutes.
3. Remove the pot from the heat and let it cool slightly.
4. In a blender, combine the avocado, cooked onion mixture, lime juice, salt, and pepper. Blend until smooth and creamy.
5. Taste and adjust seasoning if necessary.
6. Serve warm or chilled, garnished with fresh cilantro.

Mexican Avocado Tortilla Soup

This hearty, comforting tortilla soup features creamy avocado and crunchy tortilla strips, with a punch of Mexican spices. It's perfect for a quick weeknight dinner or when you're craving something satisfying.

Prep Time: 20 minutes

Ingredients:

- ✓ 2 ripe avocados, peeled and pitted
- ✓ 1 cup tortilla chips, broken into pieces
- ✓ 1 can (14 oz) diced tomatoes
- ✓ 2 cups vegetable broth
- ✓ 1 onion, chopped
- ✓ 2 garlic cloves, minced
- ✓ 1 tsp chili powder
- ✓ 1 tsp cumin
- ✓ 1/2 tsp paprika
- ✓ 1 tbsp lime juice
- ✓ Salt and pepper, to taste
- ✓ Fresh cilantro, for garnish
- ✓ Sour cream (optional), for serving

Method:

1. In a large pot, heat olive oil over medium heat. Add the chopped onion and garlic, cooking until soft, about 4 minutes.
2. Stir in the chili powder, cumin, paprika, and diced tomatoes. Cook for 2-3 minutes.
3. Pour in the vegetable broth and bring to a simmer. Let it cook for 10 minutes.
4. In a blender, combine the avocado, lime juice, salt, and pepper. Add a bit of the soup broth and blend until smooth.
5. Pour the avocado mixture back into the soup pot and stir well. Simmer for another 5 minutes.
6. Serve hot, topped with tortilla chips, fresh cilantro, and a dollop of sour cream if desired.

Avocado and Black Bean Chili

This hearty and flavorful avocado and black bean chili is a delicious twist on a classic chili. The combination of creamy avocado, protein-packed black beans, and spices creates a satisfying and nutritious dish perfect for any time of year.

Prep Time: 10 minutes Cook Time: 25 minutes

Ingredients:

- 2 ripe avocados, peeled and pitted
- 2 cans (15 oz each) black beans, drained and rinsed
- 1 can (14 oz) diced tomatoes
- 1 onion, chopped
- 1 garlic clove, minced
- 1 tbsp olive oil
- 1 tbsp chili powder
- 1 tsp cumin
- 1/2 tsp smoked paprika
- 1/2 cup vegetable broth
- Salt and pepper, to taste
- Lime juice, to taste
- Fresh cilantro, for garnish

Method:

1. Heat olive oil in a large pot over medium heat. Add the chopped onion and minced garlic, cooking until softened, about 5 minutes.
2. Stir in the chili powder, cumin, smoked paprika, and salt, and cook for another minute.
3. Add the diced tomatoes, black beans, and vegetable broth. Bring to a simmer, cooking for about 10-15 minutes to let the flavors meld together.
4. While the chili is simmering, mash the avocado in a bowl with a fork until smooth.
5. Once the chili is done, stir in the mashed avocado and lime juice. Adjust the seasoning with salt and pepper if needed.

6. Serve hot, garnished with fresh cilantro.

Avocado and Tomato Gazpacho

This chilled avocado and tomato gazpacho is a refreshing and creamy twist on the classic Spanish summer soup. With ripe tomatoes, creamy avocado, and fresh herbs, this soup is light, cool, and packed with vibrant flavors.

Prep Time: 15 minutes Chill Time: 1 hour

Ingredients:

- 2 ripe avocados, peeled and pitted
- 4 large ripe tomatoes, chopped
- 1 cucumber, peeled and chopped
- 1 small onion, chopped
- 1 garlic clove, minced
- 1/4 cup olive oil
- 2 tbsp red wine vinegar
- 1 tbsp lime juice
- 1/2 tsp ground cumin
- Salt and pepper, to taste
- Fresh basil or cilantro, for garnish

Method:

1. In a blender, combine the avocados, tomatoes, cucumber, onion, garlic, olive oil, red wine vinegar, lime juice, and cumin.
2. Blend until smooth and creamy. If the soup is too thick, add a little cold water or vegetable broth to reach your desired consistency.
3. Season with salt and pepper to taste.
4. Chill the gazpacho in the fridge for at least 1 hour before serving.
5. Serve cold, garnished with fresh basil or cilantro.

Avocado Miso Soup

This avocado miso soup brings together the earthy flavors of miso and the creaminess of avocado for a comforting, nourishing soup. It's simple to make, and the avocado adds a rich texture and freshness to the traditional Japanese soup.

Prep Time: 5 minutes Cook Time: 10 minutes

Ingredients:

- ✓ 2 ripe avocados, peeled and pitted
- ✓ 4 cups vegetable broth
- ✓ 2 tbsp white miso paste
- ✓ 1 tbsp soy sauce
- ✓ 1 tbsp sesame oil
- ✓ 1/2 tsp ground ginger
- ✓ 1/2 cup tofu cubes (optional)
- ✓ 2 green onions, chopped
- ✓ 1 tbsp sesame seeds, for garnish

Method:

1. In a medium pot, bring the vegetable broth to a simmer over medium heat. Stir in the miso paste and soy sauce, whisking to dissolve the miso.
2. Add the sesame oil and ground ginger, stirring to combine.
3. Gently add the tofu cubes (if using) and cook for 3-4 minutes until heated through.
4. While the soup is simmering, mash the avocado in a bowl until smooth.
5. Once the soup is ready, remove from heat and stir in the mashed avocado until well combined.
6. Ladle the soup into bowls, garnish with chopped green onions and sesame seeds, and serve hot.

Avocado and Roasted Pepper Soup

This vibrant avocado and roasted pepper soup is smoky, creamy, and full of flavor. The combination of roasted peppers and creamy avocado makes for a velvety smooth texture that's perfect for any occasion.

Prep Time: 10 minutes Cook Time: 25 minutes

Ingredients:

- ✓ 2 ripe avocados, peeled and pitted
- ✓ 2 red bell peppers, roasted and peeled
- ✓ 1 onion, chopped
- ✓ 2 garlic cloves, minced
- ✓ 1 tbsp olive oil
- ✓ 2 cups vegetable broth
- ✓ 1/2 tsp smoked paprika
- ✓ Salt and pepper, to taste
- ✓ Lime juice, to taste
- ✓ Fresh cilantro, for garnish

Method:

1. Heat the olive oil in a large pot over medium heat. Add the chopped onion and garlic, cooking until softened, about 5 minutes.
2. Add the roasted red peppers, vegetable broth, smoked paprika, salt, and pepper. Bring the mixture to a simmer and cook for about 10 minutes.
3. Remove the pot from heat and let it cool slightly.
4. In a blender, combine the avocado and the roasted pepper mixture. Blend until smooth and creamy.
5. Taste and adjust seasoning with salt, pepper, and lime juice.
6. Serve hot, garnished with fresh cilantro.

Avocado and Chicken Soup

This avocado and chicken soup is comforting, hearty, and packed with protein. The creamy avocado adds a luxurious texture to the chicken broth, making it the perfect dish for cozy nights or a quick meal.

Prep Time: 15 minutes Cook Time: 30 minutes

Ingredients:

- 2 ripe avocados, peeled and pitted
- 2 chicken breasts, cooked and shredded
- 4 cups chicken broth
- 1 onion, chopped
- 2 garlic cloves, minced
- 1 tbsp olive oil
- 1 tsp ground cumin
- 1/2 tsp chili powder
- 1/2 tsp paprika
- 1 tbsp lime juice
- Salt and pepper, to taste
- Fresh cilantro, for garnish

Method:

1. Heat olive oil in a large pot over medium heat. Add the chopped onion and garlic, cooking until softened, about 5 minutes.
2. Stir in the cumin, chili powder, paprika, salt, and pepper, and cook for another minute.
3. Add the chicken broth and bring to a simmer. Let it cook for 10-15 minutes to allow the flavors to meld.
4. While the broth is simmering, mash the avocado in a bowl until smooth.
5. Once the soup is ready, stir in the shredded chicken and mashed avocado. Simmer for another 5 minutes until heated through.
6. Add lime juice and adjust seasoning if necessary.
7. Serve hot, garnished with fresh cilantro.

Grilled Avocado with Lime and Salt

Grilled avocado with lime and salt is a simple yet delicious dish that brings out the creamy richness of the avocado while adding a smoky flavor. The tangy lime and a pinch of salt enhance the natural taste, making it an easy and satisfying appetizer or side dish.

Prep Time: 5 minutes Cook Time: 5 minutes

Ingredients:

- ✓ 2 ripe avocados, halved and pitted
- ✓ 1 tbsp olive oil
- ✓ 1 lime, cut into wedges
- ✓ Salt, to taste
- ✓ Pepper, to taste

Method:

1. Preheat the grill to medium heat.
2. Lightly brush the cut sides of the avocado halves with olive oil.
3. Place the avocado halves on the grill, flesh-side down. Grill for 2-3 minutes or until grill marks appear.
4. Remove from the grill and sprinkle with salt and pepper.
5. Squeeze fresh lime juice over the grilled avocados before serving.
6. Serve immediately, garnished with extra lime wedges.

Baked Avocado with Egg

Baked avocado with egg is a healthy, delicious, and satisfying breakfast or brunch option. The avocado becomes perfectly creamy when baked, and the egg provides a wonderful protein boost. It's easy to prepare and customizable with your favorite seasonings.

Prep Time: 5 minutes Cook Time: 15 minutes

Ingredients:

- ✓ 2 ripe avocados, halved and pitted
- ✓ 2 eggs
- ✓ Salt and pepper, to taste
- ✓ Red pepper flakes (optional)
- ✓ Fresh herbs (optional, such as chives or parsley)

Method:

1. Preheat the oven to 375°F (190°C).
2. Scoop out a small portion of the avocado from the center to make room for the egg.
3. Place the avocado halves on a baking sheet lined with parchment paper.
4. Crack an egg into the center of each avocado half.
5. Season with salt, pepper, and red pepper flakes (if using).
6. Bake for 12-15 minutes, or until the egg whites are set but the yolk is still runny.
7. Garnish with fresh herbs before serving.

Avocado-Stuffed Chicken Breast

Avocado-stuffed chicken breast is a savory, filling dish that combines the rich, creamy texture of avocado with the tender, juicy chicken. It's an easy recipe that's perfect for a weeknight dinner or a special occasion.

Prep Time: 10 minutes Cook Time: 25 minutes

Ingredients:

- 2 boneless, skinless chicken breasts
- 1 ripe avocado, peeled, pitted, and mashed
- 1/4 cup shredded mozzarella cheese
- 1 tbsp lime juice
- Salt and pepper, to taste
- 1 tbsp olive oil
- 1/2 tsp garlic powder

Method:

1. Preheat the oven to 375°F (190°C).
2. Slice a pocket into each chicken breast, being careful not to cut all the way through.
3. In a small bowl, mix the mashed avocado, mozzarella cheese, lime juice, salt, and pepper.
4. Stuff each chicken breast with the avocado mixture.
5. Heat olive oil in a skillet over medium-high heat. Sear the chicken breasts for 2-3 minutes per side until golden brown.
6. Transfer the chicken to the oven and bake for 20 minutes or until the chicken is cooked through.
7. Serve hot, garnished with extra lime wedges.

Roasted Avocado and Sweet Potato

Roasted avocado and sweet potato make for a perfect side dish or even a light main course. The sweet, caramelized flavors of the roasted sweet potatoes complement the creamy avocado, creating a satisfying and nutritious dish.

Prep Time: 10 minutes Cook Time: 30 minutes

Ingredients:

- 2 ripe avocados, halved and pitted
- 2 medium sweet potatoes, peeled and cut into cubes
- 1 tbsp olive oil
- 1 tsp smoked paprika
- Salt and pepper, to taste
- Fresh cilantro, for garnish

Method:

1. Preheat the oven to 400°F (200°C).
2. Toss the sweet potato cubes with olive oil, smoked paprika, salt, and pepper.
3. Spread the sweet potatoes on a baking sheet and roast for 20-25 minutes, flipping halfway through, until tender.
4. During the last 5 minutes of roasting, place the avocado halves on the baking sheet, cut side down, and roast until lightly browned.
5. Serve the roasted sweet potatoes and avocado halves together, garnished with fresh cilantro.

Grilled Avocado and Cheese Skewers

Grilled avocado and cheese skewers are a fun and flavorful appetizer. The smoky grilled avocado pairs perfectly with the melty cheese, creating a savory treat that's sure to please any crowd.

Prep Time: 5 minutes Cook Time: 5 minutes

Ingredients:

- ✓ 2 ripe avocados, peeled, pitted, and cut into cubes
- ✓ 8 oz mozzarella cheese, cut into cubes
- ✓ 1 tbsp olive oil
- ✓ Salt and pepper, to taste
- ✓ 1 tbsp balsamic glaze (optional)

Method:

1. Preheat the grill to medium heat.
2. Thread the avocado cubes and cheese cubes onto skewers, alternating between the two.
3. Brush the skewers with olive oil and season with salt and pepper.
4. Grill the skewers for 2-3 minutes per side until the cheese starts to melt and the avocado has grill marks.
5. Serve with a drizzle of balsamic glaze if desired.

BBQ Avocado and Corn

BBQ avocado and corn combine the sweetness of grilled corn with the creamy richness of avocado. This dish makes a perfect side or topping for tacos, and it's full of smoky, tangy flavors.

Prep Time: 10 minutes Cook Time: 15 minutes

Ingredients:

- 2 ripe avocados, peeled and pitted
- 2 ears of corn, husked
- 1 tbsp olive oil
- Salt and pepper, to taste
- 1 tbsp lime juice
- 1/4 tsp chili powder (optional)

Method:

1. Preheat the grill to medium heat.
2. Brush the corn with olive oil and season with salt and pepper. Grill for 10-12 minutes, rotating occasionally, until the kernels are charred.
3. While the corn is grilling, cut the avocado into chunks.
4. Once the corn is done, remove it from the grill and cut the kernels off the cob.
5. In a bowl, combine the grilled corn and avocado. Drizzle with lime juice and sprinkle with chili powder if using.
6. Serve warm as a side dish or topping.

Avocado-Stuffed Mushrooms

Avocado-stuffed mushrooms are a delightful appetizer or side dish. The creamy avocado filling pairs perfectly with the earthy mushrooms, making it a great option for a light meal or party platter.

Prep Time: 10 minutes Cook Time: 15 minutes

Ingredients:

- ✓ 12 large mushroom caps, stems removed
- ✓ 1 ripe avocado, peeled and pitted
- ✓ 1 tbsp lime juice
- ✓ 1 tbsp fresh cilantro, chopped
- ✓ Salt and pepper, to taste

Method:

1. Preheat the oven to 375°F (190°C).
2. Place the mushroom caps on a baking sheet.
3. In a bowl, mash the avocado with lime juice, cilantro, salt, and pepper.
4. Stuff each mushroom cap with the avocado mixture.
5. Bake for 12-15 minutes, or until the mushrooms are tender.
6. Serve immediately, garnished with extra cilantro.

Avocado and Halloumi Skewers

Avocado and halloumi skewers are a perfect pairing of creamy avocado and salty, grilled halloumi cheese. The contrast of textures and flavors makes these skewers a crowd-pleasing dish for any occasion.

Prep Time: 10 minutes Cook Time: 5 minutes

Ingredients:

- ✓ 2 ripe avocados, peeled, pitted, and cut into cubes
- ✓ 8 oz halloumi cheese, cut into cubes
- ✓ 1 tbsp olive oil
- ✓ 1 tbsp lemon juice
- ✓ Salt and pepper, to taste

Method:

1. Preheat the grill to medium heat.
2. Thread the avocado cubes and halloumi cheese cubes onto skewers.
3. Brush the skewers with olive oil and season with salt and pepper.
4. Grill for 2-3 minutes per side until the halloumi cheese is golden and the avocado is slightly charred.
5. Drizzle with lemon juice before serving.

Baked Avocado Parmesan Fries

Baked avocado Parmesan fries are a healthier twist on traditional fries. The creamy avocado is coated in Parmesan cheese and breadcrumbs, then baked to golden perfection, making them crispy on the outside and soft on the inside.

Prep Time: 10 minutes Cook Time: 20 minutes

Ingredients:

- ✓ 2 ripe avocados, peeled and pitted
- ✓ 1/2 cup grated Parmesan cheese
- ✓ 1/2 cup breadcrumbs
- ✓ 1/2 tsp garlic powder
- ✓ Salt and pepper, to taste
- ✓ 1 egg, beaten

Method:

1. Preheat the oven to 400°F (200°C).
2. Cut the avocados into fries or wedges.
3. In a bowl, combine the Parmesan cheese, breadcrumbs, garlic powder, salt, and pepper.
4. Dip each avocado wedge into the beaten egg, then coat with the breadcrumb mixture.
5. Place the avocado fries on a baking sheet lined with parchment paper.
6. Bake for 15-20 minutes, flipping halfway through, until golden and crispy.
7. Serve with your favorite dipping sauce.

Grilled Avocado with Honey Glaze

Grilled avocado with honey glaze is a sweet and savory dish that makes a unique appetizer or side. The honey glaze caramelizes on the grill, creating a delightful contrast with the creamy avocado.

Prep Time: 5 minutes Cook Time: 5 minutes

Ingredients:

- 2 ripe avocados, halved and pitted
- 2 tbsp honey
- 1 tbsp olive oil
- Salt, to taste

Method:

1. Preheat the grill to medium heat.
2. Brush the cut sides of the avocados with olive oil.
3. Grill the avocados, cut side down, for 2-3 minutes.
4. In a small bowl, mix the honey with a pinch of salt.
5. Drizzle the honey glaze over the grilled avocados.
6. Serve immediately as a sweet and savory treat.

Avocado Banana Smoothie

The avocado banana smoothie combines the creamy richness of avocado with the natural sweetness of banana. This nutrient-packed drink is perfect for breakfast or a post-workout snack, providing healthy fats and energy.

Prep Time: 5 minutes Cook Time: None

Ingredients:

- 1 ripe avocado, peeled and pitted
- 1 ripe banana, peeled
- 1 cup milk (or plant-based milk)
- 1 tbsp honey or maple syrup (optional)
- Ice cubes (optional)

Method:

1. Add the avocado, banana, and milk into a blender.
2. Blend until smooth and creamy.
3. Taste and add honey or maple syrup if more sweetness is desired.
4. If you prefer a chilled smoothie, add a few ice cubes and blend again.
5. Pour into a glass and serve immediately.

Avocado and Chocolate Milkshake

Avocado and chocolate milkshake is a creamy and indulgent treat that combines the richness of avocado with the sweetness of chocolate. It's a perfect dessert or refreshing drink for chocolate lovers.

Prep Time: 5 minutes Cook Time: None

Ingredients:

- 1 ripe avocado, peeled and pitted
- 1 cup chocolate milk (or regular milk with 2 tbsp cocoa powder)
- 1-2 tbsp honey or sugar (optional)
- 1/2 tsp vanilla extract (optional)
- Ice cubes (optional)

Method:

1. Add the avocado, chocolate milk, honey, and vanilla extract to a blender.
2. Blend until smooth and creamy.
3. If you want a colder milkshake, add ice cubes and blend again.
4. Pour into a glass and enjoy!

Avocado Matcha Latte

Avocado matcha latte is a unique and creamy twist on the traditional matcha latte. The avocado adds a smooth texture, while the matcha provides an earthy flavor, making this drink perfect for a boost of energy with a rich, creamy consistency.

Prep Time: 5 minutes Cook Time: None

Ingredients:

- 1 ripe avocado, peeled and pitted
- 1 tsp matcha powder
- 1 cup milk (or plant-based milk)
- 1 tbsp honey or sweetener of choice
- Ice cubes (optional)

Method:

1. In a small bowl, whisk the matcha powder with a little hot water until it's fully dissolved.
2. Add the matcha mixture, avocado, milk, and honey to a blender.
3. Blend until smooth and creamy.
4. If you want an iced version, add ice cubes and blend again.
5. Pour into a glass and serve immediately.

Avocado and Coconut Smoothie

Avocado and coconut smoothie is a tropical, creamy drink that combines the rich texture of avocado with the refreshing flavor of coconut. It's the perfect pick-me-up for a hot day or a nourishing breakfast.

Prep Time: 5 minutes Cook Time: None

Ingredients:

- ✓ 1 ripe avocado, peeled and pitted
- ✓ 1/2 cup coconut milk
- ✓ 1/2 cup water or coconut water
- ✓ 1 tbsp shredded coconut (optional)
- ✓ Ice cubes (optional)

Method:

1. Add the avocado, coconut milk, water or coconut water, and shredded coconut to a blender.
2. Blend until smooth and creamy.
3. Add ice cubes for a chilled version, and blend again.
4. Pour into a glass and garnish with extra shredded coconut if desired.

Avocado and Pineapple Juice

Avocado and pineapple juice is a tropical, refreshing beverage that combines the creamy avocado with the tangy sweetness of pineapple. This drink is packed with vitamins and makes a perfect start to your day or a refreshing afternoon treat.

Prep Time: 5 minutes Cook Time: None

Ingredients:

- ✓ 1 ripe avocado, peeled and pitted
- ✓ 1 cup fresh pineapple chunks (or pineapple juice)
- ✓ 1/2 cup cold water
- ✓ 1 tsp honey or sweetener of choice (optional)
- ✓ Ice cubes (optional)

Method:

1. Add the avocado, pineapple chunks, water, and honey to a blender.
2. Blend until smooth and creamy.
3. Add ice cubes for a colder drink and blend again.
4. Pour into a glass and serve immediately.

Iced Avocado Coffee

Iced avocado coffee is a unique blend of creamy avocado and strong coffee, making it a perfect beverage for coffee lovers who want something extra creamy with a refreshing twist.

Prep Time: 5 minutes Cook Time: None

Ingredients:

- 1 ripe avocado, peeled and pitted
- 1 cup chilled brewed coffee
- 1 tbsp sweetened condensed milk or regular milk
- Ice cubes

Method:

1. Add the avocado, chilled coffee, and sweetened condensed milk to a blender.
2. Blend until smooth and creamy.
3. Pour the mixture over a glass filled with ice cubes.
4. Stir well and serve immediately.

Avocado and Almond Butter Smoothie

Avocado and almond butter smoothie combines the creaminess of avocado with the nutty richness of almond butter. This smoothie is packed with healthy fats and protein, making it a great option for a filling breakfast or post-workout snack.

Prep Time: 5 minutes Cook Time: None

Ingredients:

- 1 ripe avocado, peeled and pitted
- 1 tbsp almond butter
- 1 cup milk (or plant-based milk)
- 1 tbsp honey or maple syrup (optional)
- Ice cubes (optional)

Method:

1. Add the avocado, almond butter, milk, and honey to a blender.
2. Blend until smooth and creamy.
3. Add ice cubes if you prefer a colder smoothie and blend again.
4. Pour into a glass and enjoy immediately.

Avocado and Strawberry Lassi

Avocado and strawberry lassi is a creamy, fruity drink that blends the rich texture of avocado with the sweet tanginess of strawberries. It's a refreshing and nutritious beverage, perfect for a warm day or as a healthy snack.

Prep Time: 5 minutes Cook Time: None

Ingredients:

- ✓ 1 ripe avocado, peeled and pitted
- ✓ 1/2 cup strawberries, fresh or frozen
- ✓ 1 cup yogurt (or plant-based yogurt)
- ✓ 1 tbsp honey or sweetener of choice
- ✓ Ice cubes (optional)

Method:

1. Add the avocado, strawberries, yogurt, and honey to a blender.
2. Blend until smooth and creamy.
3. Add ice cubes for a chilled version and blend again.
4. Pour into a glass and serve immediately.

Green Detox Avocado Smoothie

Green detox avocado smoothie combines the creamy richness of avocado with the refreshing taste of greens like spinach and cucumber. It's packed with antioxidants and nutrients, making it a great detox drink to start your day.

Prep Time: 5 minutes Cook Time: None

Ingredients:

- 1 ripe avocado, peeled and pitted
- 1/2 cup spinach leaves (or kale)
- 1/2 cucumber, peeled and chopped
- 1 cup coconut water or plain water
- 1 tbsp lemon juice
- Ice cubes (optional)

Method:

1. Add the avocado, spinach, cucumber, coconut water, and lemon juice to a blender.
2. Blend until smooth and creamy.
3. Add ice cubes for a chilled smoothie and blend again.
4. Pour into a glass and serve immediately.

Avocado and Chia Milkshake

Avocado and chia milkshake is a creamy, nutritious drink that combines the healthy fats of avocado with the fiber-rich chia seeds. It's perfect for a filling snack or a boost of energy in the morning.

Prep Time: 5 minutes Cook Time: None

Ingredients:

- ✓ 1 ripe avocado, peeled and pitted
- ✓ 1 tbsp chia seeds
- ✓ 1 cup milk (or plant-based milk)
- ✓ 1 tbsp honey or maple syrup (optional)
- ✓ Ice cubes (optional)

Method:

1. Add the avocado, chia seeds, milk, and honey to a blender.
2. Blend until smooth and creamy.
3. If you want a colder milkshake, add ice cubes and blend again.
4. Pour into a glass and let the chia seeds soak for a few minutes before serving.

Avocado Chocolate Mousse

Avocado chocolate mousse is a creamy, velvety dessert that's naturally sweetened and packed with healthy fats. The avocado gives this mousse its rich, smooth texture while the chocolate provides the perfect indulgence.

Prep Time: 10 minutes Cook Time: None

Ingredients:

- 1 ripe avocado, peeled and pitted
- 1/4 cup cocoa powder
- 1/4 cup maple syrup or honey
- 1/4 cup coconut milk (or any milk of choice)
- 1 tsp vanilla extract
- Pinch of salt
- 1/4 cup dark chocolate chips (optional, for extra richness)

Method:

1. In a blender or food processor, combine the avocado, cocoa powder, maple syrup, coconut milk, vanilla extract, and a pinch of salt.
2. Blend until smooth and creamy. If desired, melt the chocolate chips and stir them into the mousse for an extra chocolatey flavor.
3. Taste and adjust sweetness if necessary.
4. Spoon into small cups or bowls and refrigerate for at least 1 hour before serving.
5. Garnish with grated chocolate, berries, or whipped cream if desired.

Avocado and Coconut Ice Cream

Avocado and coconut ice cream is a tropical, dairy-free treat with a silky texture. The avocado provides a creamy base, while the coconut adds a rich, aromatic flavor. Perfect for a refreshing dessert!

Prep Time: 10 minutes Cook Time: 4 hours (freezing time)

Ingredients:

- 1 ripe avocado, peeled and pitted
- 1 can (400ml) full-fat coconut milk
- 1/4 cup maple syrup or honey
- 1 tsp vanilla extract
- Pinch of salt
- 1/2 cup shredded coconut (optional)

Method:

1. Blend the avocado, coconut milk, maple syrup, vanilla extract, and salt in a blender until smooth.
2. Pour the mixture into a container, stirring in the shredded coconut if using.
3. Freeze for at least 4 hours, or until the ice cream is firm.
4. Let the ice cream sit at room temperature for a few minutes before scooping and serving.

Avocado Brownies

Avocado brownies are rich, fudgy, and made healthier with avocado. The avocado replaces butter or oil while still giving the brownies a dense and moist texture, without sacrificing the delicious chocolate flavor.

Prep Time: 15 minutes Cook Time: 25 minutes

Ingredients:

- 1 ripe avocado, peeled and pitted
- 1/2 cup cocoa powder
- 1/2 cup sugar (or sweetener of choice)
- 1/2 cup flour (or almond flour for a gluten-free option)
- 2 eggs
- 1 tsp vanilla extract
- 1/4 tsp baking soda
- Pinch of salt
- 1/4 cup dark chocolate chips (optional)

Method:

1. Preheat the oven to 350°F (175°C) and grease a baking pan or line with parchment paper.
2. In a bowl, mash the avocado until smooth. Mix in the eggs, vanilla extract, sugar, and baking soda.
3. Stir in the cocoa powder, flour, and salt until well combined. Add chocolate chips if desired.
4. Pour the batter into the prepared pan and spread evenly.
5. Bake for 20-25 minutes, or until a toothpick inserted into the center comes out mostly clean.
6. Let cool before slicing and serving.

Avocado Cheesecake

Avocado cheesecake is a light and creamy dessert that uses avocado to replace some of the traditional cream cheese. The result is a rich yet smooth texture with a subtle, earthy flavor that pairs perfectly with a graham cracker crust.

Prep Time: 15 minutes Cook Time: 1 hour (chill time)

Ingredients:

- ✓ 2 ripe avocados, peeled and pitted
- ✓ 1 package (8 oz) cream cheese, softened
- ✓ 1/4 cup honey or maple syrup
- ✓ 1 tsp vanilla extract
- ✓ 1 cup graham cracker crumbs
- ✓ 1/4 cup melted butter
- ✓ 1/4 cup coconut flour (optional)

Method:

1. Preheat the oven to 350°F (175°C). Mix the graham cracker crumbs with melted butter and press into the base of a springform pan.
2. Bake the crust for 5-7 minutes, then let it cool.
3. Blend the avocado, cream cheese, honey, and vanilla extract in a blender or food processor until smooth and creamy.
4. Pour the avocado mixture over the cooled crust and smooth out the top.
5. Chill the cheesecake in the refrigerator for at least 1 hour before serving.

Avocado and Lime Popsicles

These avocado and lime popsicles are a refreshing treat with a creamy texture and a zesty lime flavor. The avocado adds richness, while the lime provides a tangy contrast, making them perfect for hot summer days.

Prep Time: 10 minutes Cook Time: 4 hours (freezing time)

Ingredients:

- ✓ 1 ripe avocado, peeled and pitted
- ✓ 1/4 cup lime juice
- ✓ 1/2 cup coconut milk
- ✓ 2 tbsp honey or agave syrup
- ✓ 1/4 cup water (optional, for a thinner texture)

Method:

1. Blend the avocado, lime juice, coconut milk, honey, and water (if needed) until smooth.
2. Pour the mixture into popsicle molds.
3. Insert sticks and freeze for at least 4 hours, or until fully frozen.
4. Run warm water over the outside of the molds to help release the popsicles.

Avocado and Banana Muffins

Avocado and banana muffins are a nutritious and moist option for breakfast or a snack. The avocado replaces some of the fat, while the banana provides natural sweetness and moisture.

Prep Time: 10 minutes Cook Time: 20-25 minutes

Ingredients:

- 1 ripe avocado, peeled and pitted
- 1 ripe banana, mashed
- 1 cup flour (or almond flour for gluten-free)
- 1/4 cup sugar (or sweetener of choice)
- 1/2 tsp baking powder
- 1/4 tsp baking soda
- 1/4 tsp cinnamon (optional)
- 1 egg
- 1/4 cup milk (or plant-based milk)

Method:

1. Preheat the oven to 350°F (175°C) and grease a muffin tin.
2. Mash the avocado and banana in a large bowl.
3. Mix in the egg, milk, sugar, baking powder, baking soda, and cinnamon.
4. Stir in the flour until well combined.
5. Pour the batter into the muffin tin and bake for 20-25 minutes, or until a toothpick comes out clean.
6. Let cool before serving.

Avocado Pancakes with Maple Syrup

These avocado pancakes are fluffy and delicious, with avocado adding moisture and richness. Topped with maple syrup, they make for a satisfying breakfast or brunch.

Prep Time: 10 minutes Cook Time: 15 minutes

Ingredients:

- 1 ripe avocado, peeled and pitted
- 1 cup flour
- 1 tbsp baking powder
- 1/2 tsp salt
- 1 egg
- 1/2 cup milk (or plant-based milk)
- 2 tbsp melted butter or oil
- Maple syrup, for serving

Method:

1. Mash the avocado in a large bowl.
2. Add the flour, baking powder, salt, egg, milk, and melted butter. Stir to combine.
3. Heat a skillet over medium heat and lightly grease it.
4. Pour about 1/4 cup of batter onto the skillet and cook until bubbles appear on the surface, about 2-3 minutes. Flip and cook for another 1-2 minutes.
5. Serve with maple syrup and enjoy!

Avocado and Mango Sorbet

This avocado and mango sorbet is a refreshing, naturally sweet treat with a creamy texture. The avocado helps create a smooth, velvety sorbet that pairs beautifully with the tropical sweetness of mango.

Prep Time: 10 minutes Cook Time: 4 hours (freezing time)

Ingredients:

- ✓ 1 ripe avocado, peeled and pitted
- ✓ 1 ripe mango, peeled and chopped
- ✓ 1/4 cup lime juice
- ✓ 1/4 cup honey or maple syrup
- ✓ 1/2 cup water

Method:

1. Blend the avocado, mango, lime juice, honey, and water until smooth.
2. Pour the mixture into a shallow dish and freeze for at least 4 hours.
3. Use a fork to scrape the sorbet every 30 minutes until it reaches a fluffy consistency.
4. Serve scoops of the sorbet when ready.

Avocado Matcha Cake

Avocado matcha cake is a soft, fluffy cake that blends the creamy texture of avocado with the earthy flavor of matcha. It's a delicious and slightly healthier option for those who love green tea desserts.

Prep Time: 15 minutes Cook Time: 30-35 minutes

Ingredients:

- 1 ripe avocado, peeled and pitted
- 1 cup flour
- 2 tbsp matcha powder
- 1 tsp baking powder
- 1/2 cup sugar (or sweetener of choice)
- 1/4 cup milk (or plant-based milk)
- 2 eggs
- 1/4 cup butter, melted

Method:

1. Preheat the oven to 350°F (175°C) and grease a cake pan.
2. Blend the avocado, eggs, milk, and sugar until smooth.
3. In a separate bowl, mix the flour, matcha powder, and baking powder.
4. Combine the wet and dry ingredients, then fold in the melted butter.
5. Pour the batter into the prepared pan and bake for 30-35 minutes, or until a toothpick comes out clean.
6. Let cool before serving.

Avocado and Honey Pudding

This creamy avocado and honey pudding is a naturally sweet, rich dessert. With avocado as the base, it's a healthier alternative to traditional pudding, while still delivering indulgent flavor.

Prep Time: 5 minutes Cook Time: None

Ingredients:

- ✓ 1 ripe avocado, peeled and pitted
- ✓ 2 tbsp honey or maple syrup
- ✓ 1 tsp vanilla extract
- ✓ 1/4 cup milk (or plant-based milk)
- ✓ Pinch of salt

Method:

1. Blend the avocado, honey, vanilla extract, milk, and salt until smooth.
2. Taste and adjust sweetness as needed.
3. Spoon into small bowls or jars and refrigerate for at least 1 hour.
4. Serve chilled with berries or whipped cream if desired.

Made in the USA
Las Vegas, NV
03 April 2025